# SEASONS OF THE
# ELK

D1367036

**NorthWord**
**WILDLIFE SERIES**

# DEDICATION

For Mary Jo.
How she puts up with my single-mindedness as I write,
I'll never know. But I am grateful.


# ACKNOWLEDGMENTS

I want to thank Dave Stalling, conservation writer for the Rocky Mountain Elk Foundation for helping me round up so much good biological and historical information on elk. Thanks also to the various biologists from western elk states for forwarding similar material to me, and who often work unrecognized for the betterment of elk under less than ideal staff and budget situations.

To the members and staff of the Rocky Mountain Elk Foundation, I must also send my thanks. What you do for that which you love is a grand and glorious thing.

© Michael Furtman, 1997
Photography © Stan Osolinski/Dembinsky Photo Associates, 1997

NorthWord Press, Inc.
P.O. Box 1360
Minocqua, WI 54548

Book design by Kenneth Hey

For a free catalog describing our audio products, nature books and calendars, call **1-800-356-4465**, or write Consumer Inquiries, NorthWord Press, Inc., P.O. Box 1360, Minocqua, Wisconsin 54548.


**Library of Congress Cataloging-in-Publication Data**
Furtman, Michael.
    Seasons of the elk / by Michael Furtman ; photography
by Stanley Osolinski.
        p.   cm. — (NorthWord wildlife series)
    ISBN 1-55971-586-3 (sc)
    1. Elk.   I. Osolinski, Stan.   II. Title.   III. Series.
QL737.U55F86   1997
599.65'42—dc21                    96-37141


Printed in Singapore

# SEASONS OF THE
# ELK

by Michael Furtman

photography by Stan Osolinski

NORTHWORD

NORTHWORD PRESS, INC.
Minocqua, Wisconsin

# CONTENTS

# NEWCOMERS, BOTH

The association between humans and elk has indeed been a long one. Mostly it has been one of hunter and the hunted, although there is little doubt that humans have also long sensed the elk's majesty and beauty. We've benefited much by their presence.

It was in Beringia—the land bridge between Siberia and North America—that both men and elk wandered in search of their respective needs. Beringia appeared whenever glaciers had so much of the world's water locked up as ice that the sea levels dropped. Human predation of elk may have had some small influence on the why and when of elk migration to North America. The elk's defense mechanism is to flee, and sometimes they flee great distances—from one mountain valley to the next—when pressured by people.

People have long recognized the majesty of elk.

Archeological evidence found in
Alaska proves that hunters sat on ridge
tops to watch for migrating game
animals, huddled around small fires
and slowly, carefully chipping away at
the flint they had carried there, crafting
beautiful and sharp stone tips for
their weapons.

The time was the end of the
Pleistocene epoch—the end of the Ice
Age. Picture a world much as we know
it today, but clean, pure, new. Salmon
in unimaginable numbers choked clear
rivers during spawning runs. Herds of
plains animals drifted like dusty clouds
across each continent's grasslands.
Forests, ancient, dark and tall climbed
mountains and clung to shorelines.
The last of the mastodons and
mammoths still lumbered in our world.
People, mobile, crafty and hardy, were
much then as we are today. Most were
wanderers, probing intelligently into
every corner of the globe. Only in a few
parts of the world had we begun experi-
menting with agriculture, and the only animal we had yet domesticated
was the wolf, which became our dog. Although those that pursued elk
and other animals across Beringia were not as "advanced" as were the
Native Americans (which they became) at the time of European contact,
if you were to picture a similar lifestyle, you would have a feel for the
lives of these hunters.

After the last Ice Age, elk adapted to a wide range
of North American habitats.

Elk, too, have not changed much since that time. Theirs had been
a thirty-five-million-year-long evolutionary course from much smaller,
tropical deer-like creatures, and the ten or so thousand years between
the end of the last ice age is just the smallest blip on a chart of geologic
time. And the lineage of the elk is older than our human ancestors by
as much as thirty million years.

Elk migrated to North America over the Bering land bridge.

By the time of the Pleistocene, elk were elk. Perhaps if we could go back in time we'd notice some differences (some evidence indicates they were larger), but I doubt that anyone familiar with today's elk would fail to recognize this period's ancestral form. Either these animals spread both east and west after evolving on the plateaus of Beringia, or they had already become "elk" before ever entering that land bridge; for today, elk are found both in North America and in Siberia, and other

parts of Asia. Virtually identical to those we see here in North America, these elk are found from northern Mongolia to the Transbaikalia and the Atlai Mountains of Russia, proving a common ancestry.

Besides humans and elk, other animals we often think of as native to North America crossed the land bridge before the glaciers withered, flooding this region. Grizzly bears, wolves, bison and moose wandered to the shores, and would eventually prosper as the gateway glaciers, which blocked southward migration from Alaska to the mid-latitudes, melted. Once to the south they would find a land that was nearly, and strangely, vacant—much of its native fauna having mysteriously disappeared around this time. Perhaps even the newcomers were responsible for the decline of native species. Some speculate that early humans hunted them all into extinction, a claim I must dismiss. Others speculate that the newcomers may have carried with them parasites or diseases to which they had evolved immunity, sicknesses that finished off species already declining due to a change in climate.

Whatever the cause, much of North America's wildlife declined rapidly into extinction. Much, but not all. The white-tailed deer, a true native of North America, may have browsed within sight of mastodons, mammoths, horses, camels and ground sloths, and it may have been preyed upon by lions, saber-toothed cats, dire wolves and giant bears. But these creatures, unlike the whitetail, took the permanent path of extinction, leaving a landscape in which the whitetail could flourish, and ecological niches empty for the Asian newcomers that joined them.

Fossil evidence does seem to indicate that perhaps the elk as we know it most recently evolved from a forest-dwelling ancestor of eastern Asia, an ancestor that moved onto the grassy land bridge of Beringia. From here the elk pioneered into Alaska, and then southward. But it also moved west, back across the evolving Ice Age grasslands of Asia and Europe. This ecological feature was known as the Mammoth Steppe—cold grasslands spreading from Alaska to England across Asia and Europe—and here the elk probably did mingle with the "mega fauna" of that era—the mastodons and mammoths, horses and bison. These cold-adapted elk spawned enormous variants, including the British "cave stag" that rivaled the Irish elk or the biggest bull moose in size.

It is interesting to contemplate that an animal we now associate with mountains probably evolved on a grassy plain. And it is equally fascinating to ponder that the place of the elk's origin lays awash beneath three or four hundred feet of water. Thanks to many who have spent decades studying the elk, we know much about them, but our view is only a "snapshot" of what this animal is today. Archeology has provided us with only a few scratched and faded glimpses of its past. Until we invent a time machine, the fine details of its evolution will remain a mystery.

Which is fine. For what would life be without awe? How poor our race would be if we were forever denied the chance to hear the calliope of wildness that is the bugle of a lovelorn bull, never again able to immerse our senses in this passion play called the rut, forbidden to smell the pungent power of his wallow, or to see him tend his nervous cows.

The elk is the most advanced of the Old World deer.

Next Page: Having evolved on open grasslands, the elk is a creature of meadows, prairies and plains.

Some of us still hunt, and, like our ancestors, join the elk at a molecular level, absorbing the sun's energy through a sun-to-grass-to-elk-to-human conduit. Some of us only see such scenes from the seat of the car while driving the roads of Yellowstone; yet we all come away enriched.

We should think of this and be aware that the elk—an opportunistic species that once flourished across this continent and was found in nearly every state and province—is much diminished in range and numbers today.

And we should also be aware that of the newcomers that traveled with elk to this continent, we are the only ones that can ensure its future. Fortunately, although there are fewer of them and less space in which they can live, elk are still numerous, their populations growing. Advocates like those at the Rocky Mountain Elk Foundation continue to push the elk's cause, working to return elk to places where they have not been seen in a hundred years. But more important to their future than these translocations is the protection of the last of North America's wild lands. Elk need wild places, big places, places to live and feed and fight mating battles and give birth. Conservationists continue to fight to protect elk habitat—without which elk will only exist in zoos and parks.

Elk are herd animals.

The elk is a marvelous, adaptable species. Its near future prospects are good. As fellow travelers in time and wanderers of continents, we owe it a place to thrive and the chance to continue its long evolutionary course. We are newcomers, both, to this continent.

Elk society and elk behavior is often as complex as our own. Given half a chance, elk will prosper, well endowed as they are to survive in the wild places of this continent.

Next Page: The presence of elk in the wild enriches all our lives.

# OF TIME AND PLACE

It might come as a surprise that elk were once found in almost every state and province in the United States and Canada. Their range, at the time of European settlement, may have exceeded that of the white-tailed deer, the latter often considered to be this continent's most adaptable deer. Perhaps we should have saved that title for the elk, the most highly evolved and adaptable of the Old World deer.

If the modern elk originated on Beringia, its early evolution certainly didn't take place there, nor has it stood still since the end of the last ice age, either in distance or biology. As elk spread southward into the newly warming North American continent, it encountered a wide range of habitats. Over the course of time, it managed to adapt to nearly all of them—save the semi-tropical, which isn't surprising since it began as a cold-adapted animal. And again, over time, as the elk of the eastern parts of the continent adapted to the region's hardwood forests, they became slightly different from those that flourished on the prairies, or in western mountain valleys.

Elk were once found in nearly every state and province.

These elk are closely related to other members of the red deer family throughout Asia and Europe.

## GENUS *CERVUS*

As members of the genus *Cervus,* elk number among the fifteen related species found nearly worldwide. Closely related species are native to Asia, Europe, the East Indies, the Philippines, even North Africa, and have been successfully introduced elsewhere. Some other members of the red deer family are the MacNeill's stag *(C.e. macneilli),* a large deer found in the highlands of Tibet and two provinces of China; the Spanish red deer *(C.e. hispanicus)* of Spain; and the East European *(C.e. maral)* and West European *(C.e. elaphus)* red deer. Elk and their relatives are Old World deer; New World deer, such as the white-tailed, black-tailed and mule deer are members of the genus *Odocoileus.*

Other Old World deer familiar to North Americans are moose (genus *Alces*)—called "elk" in Europe; and caribou (genus *Rangifer*). While very similar in many regards, New and Old World deer do have some subtle differences, including the manner in which the foot is constructed, location of the male genitals, the manner in which males advertise for mates, and the pattern of antler growth and shedding. It does, however, seem remarkable that New and Old World deer are so similar in so many ways, considering the separate evolutionary paths taken on different continents.

Both Old and New World deer are also members of the larger Family Cervidae—animals with antlers, four-chambered ruminating stomachs, and that usually bear spotted young. There are 53 species in the family Cervidae. The cervid's four-chambered stomach is an important adaptation, for it allowed hoofed mammals to make their way out of the tropical forests, where forage was lush, onto the grass-lands and cooler northern latitudes where forage, though seasonally abundant, was often of poor quality. Grasses and woody browse are hard to digest, and the four-chambered stomach allows for fermenta-tion, a digestive tool that uses microbacterial action to squeeze out nutrients and energy.

Cervids are generally long-legged and graceful animals that are adept at running. Male cervids grow deciduous antlers—antlers that grow, then fall off, once a year—as opposed to the permanent head adornments of the bovids, such as cows and bison.

As members of *Cervus* and Cervidae, elk then also belong to the order Artiodactyla—comprised of all even-toed, hoofed mammals—which includes such diverse species as deer, antelopes, giraffes, sheep, cattle, bison and even the hippopotamus.

## CLASSIFICATION

There has been considerable debate as to whether or not the populations of elk that adapted to the various regions of North America constitute true subspecies. There has even been debate as to whether or not the elk itself is even a separate species from the closely related red deer of Asia and Europe. Don't confuse these red deer with the "elk" that are virtually identical to ours and live in parts of Siberia and Mongolia. The latter are elk—or what biologist Dr. Valerius Geist calls "advanced wapiti"— using the Native American term for this animal to avoid confusion. In other words, all elk are red deer, but not all red deer are elk.

For centuries, the animal we now call elk was considered a separate species that itself was further divided into six subspecies—those regional forms previously mentioned. For just as long, scientists generally recognized that elk were certainly similar to the red deer of Asia and Europe—a species itself divided into many subspecies—but believed elk and red deer to be separate species. Those who believed in this theory also offered the belief that elk had entered North America during an earlier ice age—perhaps 100,000 years ago—and had already migrated south into the region we today call the United States before the last ice age. Once in North America, these scientists theorized, the regional populations, cut off from Beringia by the advancement of the Wisconsonian glacier during the last ice age, evolved first into elk (from some red deer ancestor) and then into the six subspecies.

The problem with that theory seems to be evident—the presence of animals identical to our elk in Siberia and Mongolia. If elk evolved from red deer while in North America, they would have had to migrate all the way back to Asia by following the retreating Wisconsin ice sheet north, and scooting across Beringia before it was inundated with water at the end of that ice age. Or the Mongolian-Siberian elk

Scientists now consider North American elk and the Old World deer as one species.

Geologic separation over a period of time is necessary for a single species to evolve into separate subspecies.

would have had to evolve in Asia on a parallel path with the North American elk. Both events seem unlikely. The only other possibility is that some form of red deer evolved into elk in Eurasia or Beringia during one of the earlier ice ages, then spread south before the last ice age, where it was trapped in North America to undergo subspeciation. However, there is no archeological evidence of elk being in North America at that time.

Given that the Asian elk are nearly indistinguishable from those in North America, there must have been a common ancestor a very, very short time ago (geologically speaking). For this reason, some scientists now speculate that the elk as we know it evolved in the Beringia region or adjacent parts of Asia and migrated in both directions, but only during the end of the last ice age. This seems the more likely theory.

In any case, we're still left with the matter of whether or not elk and red deer are separate species. Although considered as separate species for decades, recent evidence indicates that not enough time or evolution has taken place for true speciation to occur. The concept of geologic separation over long periods of time is critical for the development of two species from one. Geologic separation insures that the gene "flow" between populations is cut off, making it impossible for evolved adaptations in one segment to flow back to the other. Given enough time, numerous small adaptive changes amount to significant differences, and the two groups become so dissimilar that they are deemed separate species.

That just doesn't seem to be the case with elk and red deer, and certainly not the case between the regional populations found in the United States and Canada. One of the commonly accepted signs indicating that two animals are no longer of the same species is the inability for cross-matings to produce fertile offspring. Since matings between elk and red deer do result in offspring fully capable of reproducing themselves, this measure alone seems to indicate that elk and the Eurasian red deer are still the same species. Furthermore, recent technological advances have allowed molecular examination of blood serum protein from the two, which further supports the theory of single speciation.

Therefore, it is commonly accepted today that our elk are members of the red deer species, albeit a subspecies. Although they are no longer exactly the same as red deer, they have not evolved for a long enough time or developed enough significant differences to be considered a separate species.

In taxonomical terms, all red deer are classified as *Cervus elaphus*. Each of the subspecies—and there are many worldwide—are further denoted by its subspecies classification. In the elk's case, they are classified as *Cervus elaphus canadensis*—or *C.e. canadensis* for short.

There are some physical differences between elk and red deer. Elk in North America and Asia tend to have larger antlers, a coat with more strongly contrasting colors, a brighter rump patch, smaller tails and larger teeth than other red deer subspecies. Elk also tend to prefer more open country, and are well suited even to life on the prairie. Bull elk have a high pitched mating "bugle," which is better suited to open country. Red deer stags, on the other hand, have a low, lion-like roar, which carries further in the thick forests they prefer.

Although it has long been believed that there are six "subspecies" of elk in North America, that concept is coming into disfavor. One of the principle debunkers of that theory is Dr. Valerius Geist, noted elk authority from Alberta. As mentioned earlier, Geist strongly suggests that the "advanced wapiti" of Mongolia and other parts of Asia, and those of North America, are really the same animal. He also insists that the regional populations of the latter, formerly recognized as subspecies, should truly be considered as "ecotypes." Ecotypes are regional variations whose differences can be explained by differences in temperature, food and terrain.

Variations in elk size and color are due to diet and environment.

Rather than concentrating on some of the differences—such as body size and antler shape—Geist suggests that we ought to be examining those things that are the same. All bull elk bugle. All have short tails and a whitish-yellow rump. And all have a neck mane. Size differences of body and antlers can be explained by diet or other environmental factors. But the bugle, the coat, the tail—these are all inheritable traits, like eye color. In taxonomy, hereditary factors are the only things that count. In North America then, the variances found in elk are due only to their environment, and therefore are ecotypes.

## EASTERN ELK

Coming to America, Europeans encountered elk in amazing numbers across the breadth of the land. One of the first Europeans to see an elk was Jacques Cartier while ascending the St. Lawrence River in 1535.

Traveling as far as modern day Montreal, Cartier reported seeing great stores of Stags, Deere, Beares...." By his terminology, he was clearly differentiating between "Stags" (elk) and "Deere" (whitetails).

Early accounts indicate the population known as Eastern elk (the original *C.e. canadensis*—now extinct, but the Latin name now applied to all North American elk) ranged from near the Atlantic Coast south into the northern regions of the Gulf Coast states, north into southern Ontario and west through the forests to the prairie states from Arkansas north to Minnesota. This was an animal of the eastern deciduous forests and open valleys. It thrived in the region's mountains— like Rocky Mountain elk still thrive in the peaks of the West—as well as on the midwestern prairies. Eastern elk were abundant in the Allegheny mountains of Pennsylvania. They were reported in the Carolinas, New York, even into northern Louisiana—almost through-out the East with the possible exception of Maine, New Hampshire and Florida. Elk apparently were found as far north as southern Quebec.

In *Lives of Game Animals*, an early natural history text by Ernest Thompson Seton, a journal article written by Dr. B.S. Barton in 1806 states: "Within the memory of many persons now living, the droves of Elks which used to frequent the salines west of the river Susquehanna in Pennsylvania, were so great that for 5 or 6 miles leading to the 'licks,' the paths of these animals were as large as many of the great public roads of our country. Eighty Elks have sometimes been seen in one herd upon their march to the salines."

Although now primarily an animal of the West, elk were once common in the East.

Next Page: Of the six elk ecotypes native to North America, two are now extinct.

I have photographed paintings of elk on the ancient granite of southern Ontario just north of Lake Superior. This rock art, called "pictographs," was likely created by Ojibwe shamans within the last three hundred years. One such elk drawing occurs on the far eastern shore of sprawling Lac la Croix, a huge lake on the Minnesota–Ontario border.

Although faded, one can discern the bust of a bull elk in profile, above which a human figure stands holding a spear. About thirty miles due east, on the cliffs near where the Basswood River enters Crooked Lake is a spike bull elk, its antlers laid to the rear along its back. These drawings are clearly distinguishable as elk from the more common pictographs of caribou and moose, the other two deer species historically found in the region. Since the forest in this area is boreal, it hints that elk had even pioneered into this type of ecosystem, one that is not commonly associated with the species, again demonstrating the adaptability of this animal.

No one knows for sure when the last Eastern elk was killed, or exactly how it may have differed from the other five regional populations elsewhere in North America, but it nearly survived into the modern age when scientific wildlife management would have assured it a future. We do know that the last elk in Pennsylvania was killed in November of 1867, and that this was one of the last populations of elk in the East. It is a sad thing to contemplate that a once-abundant creature was so thoughtlessly allowed to take the abrupt road into extinction, and that if it had held out for just a few more decades, it might again have roamed in the wild.

But, happily, there are elk once again in Pennsylvania, and again in Michigan and Wisconsin, the descendants of Rocky Mountain elk transplants. Michigan's herd is large enough that the state even holds a hunting season. The Wisconsin elk are actually transplants from that

Transplanted Rocky Mountain elk have been successful in re-establishing limited eastern populations.

Michigan herd. They are currently doing well in their new home in the Chequamagon National Forest in northern Wisconsin; they have survived grueling winters, and have given birth to the first native-born elk calves to be seen in that state in a century.

## MERRIAM ELK

Another of the ecotypes of elk, and one that also is extinct, is the Merriam elk *(C.e. merriami)*. This animal ranged as far south as elk have ever been known to have ventured—from northern Arizona through much of New Mexico and well down the spine of Mexican mountain ranges in the provinces of Sonora, Chihuahua, Coahuila, Hidalgo and Durango. By 1906, hunting and competition with livestock drove the Merriam elk to extinction.

Elk were once numerous on, and well adapted to,
North America's prairies.

The Merriam was a larger than average elk, with antlers that
tended to be straighter than those of the Rocky Mountain elk.
Apparently, diet or other environmental factors contributed to the
Merriam's large size, contradicting Bergmann's Rule, which dictates
that southern animals are smaller than their northern counterparts.
Elk are once again doing well in Arizona, thanks to reintroductions
using Rocky Mountain elk stock. Interestingly, these introduced elk

also often grow to very large size, indicating that food and other habitat elements in this region produce large-bodied elk, not genetics.

## MANITOBAN ELK

Another large-bodied elk, and one with the darkest pelage (or coat), is the Manitoban *(C.e. manitobensis)* form.

This is the elk of the prairie, once found in huge numbers on the prairies of Alberta, Saskatchewan, Manitoba, both Dakotas, Minnesota, eastern Montana and Wyoming, Nebraska, Iowa, eastern Colorado, Kansas, Oklahoma and maybe parts of Texas.

It is generally thought that Eastern elk populated the prairies of those states east of the Mississippi River, although no one knows for sure, and elk certainly are capable of swimming across the river. It is likely that some mingling of races occurred wherever their ranges abutted, and possible that all the elk of the eastern prairies were Manitobans.

Although the Manitoban elk escaped extinction, it has been driven from the prairies by agriculture, greatly reducing its numbers.

Viable populations are found in several locations in Manitoba and Saskatchewan, and a small herd has become established again in North Dakota. The largest single herd is in Manitoba's Riding Mountain Provincial Park. Some five thousand elk live in and near this park, a park that served as a refuge to keep this form of elk from going the way of the Eastern and Merriam.

Another three or four thousand elk are found elsewhere in Manitoba. Saskatchewan hosts about eight thousand Manitoba elk.

North Dakota's small herd actually wandered in on its own after an absence of nearly one hundred years. Although some Rocky Mountain elk had already been transplanted to the state, the Manitobans found their way south into the state by following the Pembina River, apparently having originated in Manitoba's Spruce Woods Provincial Forest.

Minnesota's prairies once hosted Manitoban elk, but the state's elk population hovers today near thirty, a staggering decline from a population that must have measured in tens, if not hundreds, of thousands. I find these few elk very interesting because no one knows their true origin. The ranges of Manitoban and Eastern elk once met in this state where the prairie gives way to the eastern forest. In addition to these native forms, a few introductions of Rocky Mountain elk took place in 1913. The present-day Minnesota elk could be descendants of any or all of these races of elk, which raises the interesting question of whether or not the Eastern elk is truly extinct.

## TULE ELK

Another race of elk dramatically diminished in numbers—it is thought that there were once some 500,000—is the Tule elk *(C.e. nannodes)*. Originally inhabitants of California's dry prairies found in the San Joaquin and Sacramento valleys, it was driven both to near extinction and into the only remaining undeveloped land—the marshes—by the unrelenting expansion of that state's settlement. A local landowner and cattle baron, Henry Miller, sensing the Tule elk's pending extinction, provided them with refuge on his land, when, in 1874, two of his workers reported a pair in a marsh they were draining. Legend has it that these indeed were the last two Tule elk—if true, this is truly a remarkable brush with extinction. Even if more than two survived, it was but a handful, for despite twenty years of protection on Miller's ranch, the herd numbered only twenty-eight by 1895. Today there are twenty-two separate herds of Tule elk in California, with total numbers around 2,300.

The elk is once again making its presence known in places such as Pennsylvania and the Great Lakes states.

Once driven into the marshes along streams and lagoons, the physical size of the elk diminished for lack of suitable forage. These events led to both its current name—from the "tule" reeds found in the marshes—and its other name, the "dwarf elk." Actually, given adequate food, the Tule elk is only slightly smaller than the Rocky Mountain elk. And given a choice, it never would have retreated to the marshes, but continued to make its living—where it once existed in huge herds roaming alongside droves of pronghorn antelope—on the semi-arid plains of California.

## Roosevelt Elk

In the Pacific Northwest lives the fifth race of North American elk, the Roosevelt elk *(C.e. roosevelti)*. A large-bodied animal, the male's antlers are heavier than those of the Rocky Mountain elk, and tend to be crowned or webbed near the ends. This elk evolved in the lush, old-growth forests of this region, where these now-vanishing woods provided a relatively constant resource base. The Roosevelt elk population is fragmented, and exists in pockets from northern California through western Oregon, the Olympic Peninsula of Washington, onto Vancouver Island, the rugged coasts and mountains of British Columbia and even north to Afoganak Island, Alaska, where they were translocated in 1927.

A great deal of the Roosevelt elk's former range is now inhabited by humans, but enough forest reserves and parks exist for them to be in little danger of extinction for the time being. Some 5,000 Roosevelt elk live in Olympic National Park alone. However, since many of these herds migrate to avoid the region's deep snows and to take advantage of seasonal foods, further encroachment into specialized elk habitats by humans poses some threat to the long term viability of particular herds.

Elk require adequate amounts of uninhabited
space in order to flourish.

## Rocky Mountain Elk

The last of the subspecies or ecotypes is the Rocky Mountain elk
*(C.e. nelsoni).* It once thrived in all the Rocky Mountains, and still holds
its own wherever its habitat remains intact from northern New Mexico
north to British Columbia. This is the form that has been transplanted
to so many locations around the country, including Michigan and
Pennsylvania. Most of the translocated animals had their origin in
Yellowstone National Park, which for years had an active trap and trans-
fer program. The very ruggedness of the Rocky Mountains helped this
subspecies survive the settling of the West, allowing populations of elk to
find refuge from the settlers, who mainly tamed the prairies and valleys.

When President Theodore Roosevelt set aside vast acreage of western woods as our first National Forest shortly after the turn of the century, a great deal of elk habitat was permanently set aside.

Careful management of these herds has permitted the elk to prosper, and has ensured that the Rocky Mountain elk will be with us for as long as we protect its habitat. As with all the forms of elk, habitat loss poses the greatest threat to the animals' future, and conflicts continue to arise as humans move into elk country. Although the craggy mountainsides provide significant elk habitat during parts of the year—and much of that is protected to some degree in the form of National Forests and parks—elk move to lower elevations come winter. Unfortunately, this is the same "habitat" favored by humans, and the manner for resolving this conflict in the rapidly growing West has yet to be devised.

## SURVIVAL CHALLENGES

To the Plains Indians, the elk was a sign of wealth. Although secondary to the bison in importance as food, it was nonetheless cherished, especially for its hide. Particularly useful in the making of warm, winter clothing, it was also prized for making special ceremonial dress,

Native Americans valued the elk both as a source of food and raw materials.

its hide nearly white after tanning. Colorful elkskin dresses were worn by Blackfeet women for the important Sun Dance ritual. Warriors also cherished the elk, for a rawhide "shirt of mail" made from the neck of a bull elk thwarted arrows and the thrusting knives and spears of enemies.

No part of the elk went unused—fleshers, scrapers and flint knapping tools were made from various bones or antler parts. Shoulder blades made hoes for those tribes that planted corn, squash and other vegetables. Antlers were carved into spoons and digging sticks and special wedges for the splitting of firewood. Hooves and antler tips were rendered into a strong glue by some tribes, and elk rawhide was twisted into strong rope.

But no part of the elk was more valuable than its "tusks"—its upper canine teeth—with the largest, most brown-stained teeth worth the most. These round, thumb-tip sized teeth were utilized by almost all tribes in the elk's range, particularly as decorations on clothing or jewelry. Since there are but two "tusks" per elk, and not all of these were suitable for use, and because the native people did not kill elk just for these parts, they could only be obtained when an elk was killed for food. Thus, elk tusks were relatively rare, attaining the value placed on gold or pearls in other cultures. Gathered slowly—one or two at a time—the number used on a single dress might have taken decades to acquire. One early reference (in 1851) reports that an antelope robe, decorated with fifty-six elk tusks, was equal to the value of thirty horses!

Eventually the elk became a less fortuitous item of commerce, slaughtered in numbers by white market hunters assisted by some Indians. These gunners commonly took only the hide (which in the 1870s was worth seven dollars compared to four dollars for a bison's), tongue and tusks, leaving the rest to rot. Although the slaughter of elk was less visible than that of the bison, it was nearly as complete. By 1881, when most elk and almost all bison were eradicated, there were still some five thousand hide hunters scouring the West, searching out the remaining animals. It is remarkable, really, that any elk or bison survived.

Nearly every part of an elk was utilized by Native Americans as clothing, tools and food.

Next Page: Elk "tusks" were particularly valued by tribes as a sign of wealth.

Elk entering North America found a hospitable
new home awaiting them.

By 1907, it is estimated that only 41,000 elk survived, down from
a number that certainly was in the millions. Today, thanks to sound
conservation, about one million elk again roam.

The elk found a new continent awaiting it after the Ice Age. Here
in North America it prospered, moving as far south as any elk had
ever lived, eventually colonizing virtually every suitable habitat from
the Pacific to the Atlantic oceans. They served as prey not only for
wolves and bears and mountain lions, but for the native peoples as well.

And they survived for tens of thousands of years, prospering the while.

We will never know how many elk lived here when the first Europeans came ashore, but the numbers must have been vast, some estimate as high as ten million. And as little as a hundred and fifty years ago, elk were still found throughout their historic range, although already diminished in numbers in some regions—a blink of an eye in a species' history. Some forms barely escaped extinction, others walked nobly down that dark path.

Corn fields in Iowa will never again be plains of grass, dotted with elk and bison. The populated East, transected with freeways and clogged with cities, will never again echo with the music of a bull elk in rut. But there is country left in North America where elk are found, and still other places where, while the elk no longer exists, there remains habitat capable of supporting them.

It is to these challenges—protection of remaining habitat and the reintroduction of elk to their vacant homelands—that those who love elk must turn their attention.

The adaptable elk will do the rest.

# TO BE AN ELK

Watching an elk feed on a sultry summer day gives one but a sliver of a glimpse of all that it means to be an elk. Those lush days of plenty are but few in the year of an elk. Winter takes a great toll of the oldest and youngest elk, and springtime, too, can be deadly when late storms test already weakened elk. Life is not as easy as it seems in July. Throughout the year elk face challenges of weather, predators, birthing and mating—challenges that are sometimes fatal to a few but that strengthen many.

If some things in nature seem without cause, nothing in nature is without effect. Generations of elk have faced these challenges resulting in a hardy race, adaptive physiology, and a herding lifestyle that seeks to maximize both food and security.

The elk is the result of rigorous natural selection.

The adaptable elk is able to survive even the harshest of winters.

## LIFE IN THE COLD

That elk not only can survive harsh winters, but even prosper in its wake, is evidence of their long evolutionary path along the edge of the glaciers, products of our world's Ice Ages. From the Mammoth Steppe of a world long gone, to the valleys of the Rocky Mountains, to the winters of the East where they once lived, elk are at home with the cold.

You might say that it is this cold that shaped the elk. Tough climates mean sometimes equally tough forage, food that is fibrous and difficult to digest. Winters also imply spring and summer, bringing with them an abundance of foods. Seasonal abundance means animals must be good at storing fat for the lean months, and it also means that during the lush months, they have enough extra nutrition that they can produce superfluous adornments, such as antlers and contrasting coats.

In harsh climates, grazing animals must be able to feed on the most abundant, cold-adapted forage, which is generally grass. And since grass grows in the open, it means that the animal is best served by adopting herding behavior for reasons of safety and efficiency.

Finally, with that herding behavior comes the need for social order to avoid conflict among the many; and a larger brain, one capable of dealing with such social complexities. In addition to providing them the means to deal with the hierarchy and competition of a society, a large brain gives an animal the ability to be adaptable, to take advantage of new surroundings, able to pioneer into new areas.

All of these things are true of elk. Each adaptation spurred the next in a mosaic of evolved nuances beautiful to behold and intricate in design, the legacy of ruthless natural selection assuring only the most flexible, the most hardy, the smartest would survive. This is the elk—a symphony whose music is struck from chords of molecular wildness, whose notes are genes of survival.

Elk are creatures of what scientists call an "ecotone"—an area where different vegetative types meet, such as plains bordering forested hills, or prairies abutting river bottoms. We never will know how the elk of the great prairies behaved, or where they moved come winter, or even if their behavior was any different than those we are familiar with today that spend much time in forested settings. But no matter where they are found today, elk display similar physical and behavioral characteristics.

Elk, like other deer, are ruminants, with a four-chambered stomach that permits them to eat and digest their food in stages. Chewing their food only enough to swallow it, elk retreat to their beds to digest the forage. Except for when it is new and green, grass is pretty rough. Similarly, winter conditions may require that they eat browse such as twigs and bark. While bedded, they regurgitate a ball, or "bolus," of food to chew it anew, further breaking down the fibrous portions— otherwise known as cud chewing. But no amount of chewing would be enough to release the nutrients of some fibrous foods, and so

Bedded elk regurgitate a ball of food so that they can continue to chew the fibrous forage.

ruminating animals have evolved a unique process to capture essential protein and nutrients.

In the part of their digestive system called the "rumen," fermentation takes place, allowing elk to utilize these foods. Millions of microbacteria break down foods far too tough and fibrous for the likes of single-stomached animals, such as humans. This ability allows elk to subsist on a wide range of foods—grasses, forbs, woody browse, even bark—

which in turn means they can live in a wide range of places or habitats. This really is a remarkable evolutionary adaptation, albeit perhaps unexciting. But without it, there would be no elk.

This digestive ability also means that they can survive in regions that have seasons. Animals in a jungle environment, where weather is nearly constant, count upon abundant foods that are available in similar forms year-round. In fact, many jungle animals are highly specialized in diet, feeding only upon a narrow spectrum of plants. Elk must make do on foods that change with the season, and therefore are dietary generalists—lush spring and summer foods are easier to digest than winter-seared grasses or the tips of twigs, and the elk takes advantage of all.

Even the very same food—grass, for instance—changes in its texture and digestibility during the course of a year. When the foods change, so must microbacteria in the rumen, modifying both in number and chemistry, a process that only takes about three weeks. You might say that elk are adaptable thanks largely to these tiny living creatures within them. Even so, there is much in a plant-based diet that is indigestible, but ruminants such as elk are much better equipped to make use of it than non-ruminating grazers, such as horses.

While there is little vegetation that elk won't eat, including pine needles, there are definitely plants that they prefer. Important forage grasses are Idaho and rough fescues, timothy, needle-and-thread grass, bluegrasses, elk sedge and important flowering plants like sweet clover, beargrass, lupine, sweetvetch and arrowleaf groundsel. Some winter browse includes quaking aspen, serviceberry, chokecherry, bitterbrush, willow, sagebrush and mountain mahogany. Even some aquatic plants are high on the list, such as the succulent centers of cattail stems.

Elk have a more adaptable digestive system
than that of other deer.

Next Page: When possible, elk spend much
of their day near water.

Bull elk frequently feed alone.

In fact, water is an important criterion of elk habitat. While there are times when an elk can go without drinking, obtaining much of its water through the plants consumed, the fact is that those plants grow best where there is ample water. In other words, even when they're not drinking it, elk are drawn to areas where water can be found. During the warmest months, 80 percent of an elk's activity will take place within one quarter to one half mile of a permanent water source. Lactating cows especially seem to stake out their nursery area near a source of water.

The foraging strategy of bulls and cows does differ, but each strategy is designed to ensure that the individual succeeds at passing on its genes.

In order to pass on its genes, bulls must ensure they are chosen as breeders. In order to be chosen, bulls need to be big and have large racks. This means that they would be at a disadvantage competing with the herd for food. After their second year, bulls in the snow-free months move off to seek isolated sources of food, parcels that would be too small to attract a herd, but are of high quality and sufficient to support a loner. He must compromise security to obtain this forage, which leads to his large size and antlers. Cows, on the other hand, ensure their genes are passed on by obtaining maximum security for themselves when pregnant, and for their calves. The herd offers them this security and so they trade lower quality forage, and competition for it, for survival.

It might seem that evolution for life in a cold climate would have few advantages. Yet elk have become the most advanced of the race of red deer thanks to that evolution. Parasites, predators and diseases are less common in cold environs, resulting in less stress from these factors. This permits elk to put their energy into physical growth.

Cold climates, within reason, also mean seasonal abundance of food—even the barren-ground caribou flourishes in the Arctic's short summer. Since summer foods are both plentiful and relatively easy to digest, it allows bull elk to store fat, which in turn allows for the energy intense and highly ritualized mating season. The other awe-inspiring asset of elk—its antlers—also are a result of this seasonal abundance, for excess protein can be directed toward growing a large rack.

Cow elk also benefit by this abundance, directing their energy to producing both milk and large calves. The calves of herd animals need to be large to survive in a herd environment, which is why deer that live in herds, such as elk and caribou, rarely bear twins. All their reproductive energy is directed toward bearing a single calf.

Next Page: Elk usually give birth to a single calf, but on occasion are able to produce twins.

Lush forage is important to the cow's production of milk, and thus the survival of her calf.

That calf, its size, and when it is born are also influenced by life in a cold climate. Rutting and mating must occur within a specific time period, so that calves are born at a time most advantageous to their survival and growth. Born too early, calves succumb to late winter storms. Born too late, they can't grow large enough to survive the next winter. The elk's mating and birthing periods are more compressed in time than some of its red deer relatives that live in less rigorous climes.

Even among elk, those that live in warmer zones tend to have extended mating and birthing seasons.

## VISUAL DISPLAYS

The ancestral jungle deer tended to be very small and very territorial. Because antlers are a hindrance in such a setting, but because they needed to defend their territory, primitive jungle deer evolved tusks as weapons. Over the ages, as the elk's ancestors moved from the jungles and adapted to cool grassland settings, they adopted a herding mentality, which precludes territoriality.

Rather than defending a small territory against rivals, the elk's ancestors evolved means of visual display and ritualized contests.

Males still needed a way to defend themselves and to attract mates, but now they also needed to compete with each other in a manner that minimized the potential for injury. The seasonal abundance of foods gave them the needed extra nutrition to develop that feature—antlers.

In an open setting, antlers provide a visual clue to a bull's desirability as a mate and its status as a rival. The larger and more symmetrical the antlers, the easier they can be seen at a distance by both cows and rival bulls, which, among other things, is an energy saving device.

Just bobbing one's head, when it is adorned with antlers, provides a visible spectacle. And the bigger the antlers are, the more pronounced the display, because large antlers make a bigger "sweep" than small ones given the same amount of head movement. Being able to judge a rival or mate from a distance means you don't have to run all over the place getting near enough to test them—or flee from them.

This open-ground, visual display characteristic is seen in other deer as well—barren-ground caribou have very large antlers, and even those of the western mule deer tend to be higher and broader than those of its cousin, the whitetail. And when contests between near equals become inevitable, the large basket-shaped antlers serve to "catch" an opponent rather than spear him, the battle relegated to a shoving match.

## BUILT FOR SPEED

Animals adapted to the open also need a means of escaping predation. While forest dwelling deer tend to be masters at hiding, plains animals needed another means of avoiding predators. Hiding is fruitless. They tend to be big, noisy smelly animals in big, noisy, smelly groups. There is no way they can hide. When confronted with danger, herding animals have all chosen the same escape mechanism—fleeing. Elk are no different, and although a racehorse might be able to outrun an elk on a smooth track, few could keep apace of an elk on the broken ground found even on the prairie.

Elk are built for speed and distance, and have four gaits to accomplish both—the walk, trot, canter and gallop. The walk and the trot are merely different speeds of the same gait in which the legs track in diagonal pairs. The canter and the gallop are also similar to each other except for speed. They differ from the walk and trot in that at one point, all four legs are off the ground. At full gallop the back and abdominal muscles are brought into play, allowing elk to out-pace danger at its heels.

Those "heels" are cloven hooves and are actually toes. The foot of an elk begins at the first joint of the leg. Elk, and other deer, are "toe walkers," the entire lower leg is actually a specially evolved foot.

Symmetrical antlers are a visible sign of genetic and biological fitness.

Next Page: Large and visible to predators, elk are built to outrun enemies rather than hide from them.

Their cloven hooves are the center two "toes" of each foot. Located just above the hoof are "dew claws." They are the vestigial remains of the other toes. Hooves are made of keratin, a living substance that is constantly replaced as it wears, and the same material as our fingernails.

The long legs of elk are like a tightly strung bow, designed to store energy and release it with explosive strides. Long legs with small feet are also an advantage in stealth, for the narrow foot can be placed precisely and quietly. In addition, such long legs allow elk to get around in fairly deep snow, though they tend to hole-up if the snow gets much deeper than two feet.

## SENSES

Of course, before a predator can get close enough to even give chase, it must elude the elk's other defense mechanisms. Elk are constantly alert while feeding, and herd behavior increases the odds that trouble will be seen before it manifests. One or another elk in a herd is always looking up, watching the surroundings, testing the air. Yet if the herd were to bolt at every nervous nelly's bark, they'd spend more time running than eating. Nature has given them a "check list" that they run through before deciding to high-tail it out of the neighborhood—the senses of sight, hearing and smell.

At a distance, only those things that move need to be perceived (or worried about). Because of this, elk have evolved the ability to detect the slightest movement. Their eyes also provide them with a marvelous field of perception—they can see simultaneously to both sides and straight ahead. Thanks to the fact that they can rotate each eye independently, about the only place they can't see is in a narrow cone behind them. They even have binocular vision—similar to humans—when they look straight ahead. They don't, however, possess

In addition to a keen sense of smell, an elk has eyes that give it a wide field of view and the ability to detect the slightest motion.

color vision, at least not in the manner we do, although their night vision is far superior to ours. Imagine all the movement-sensitive, wide-angle eyes of a herd working together! A predator has its work cut out for it if it stands any chance at all of sneaking within a short rush of grazing elk.

Once something is seen, elk turn their attention to trying to hear it. One interesting quirk is the slight cracking noise elk make when they walk. Some researchers speculate that this auditory clue allows them to keep in touch with each other in thick cover or darkness. When an elk hears this noise, despite not being able to see what is making it, it knows that another elk is nearby, not a wolf.

Elk are able to rotate each ear separately to determine
the location of a sound's origin.

Should they suspect that it is a predator, elk can rotate their ears
separately from each other, allowing them pick up noises from different
directions. They might even be able to judge the distance to the predator
through the use of an echolocation technique, wherein the difference in
the length of time it takes a sound to reach each ear helps to pinpoint
the location of the source of the noise. With all eyes alert now, and big
sound-scooping ears rotating this way and that, a lurking predator had
better hold tight if it stands much chance of escaping detection.

Finally, like other deer species, elk have a highly evolved sense of
smell, used not only to detect predators, but to communicate with each
other. Scent glands located around the body produce mysterious chemical

substances called pheromones that act as an olfactory alphabet for the language of smell. These odors help elk identify individuals, act as clues to one's readiness or fitness to breed, and may even allow them to warn each other of impending danger. After first seeing something move and being on the alert elk are cautious, but not necessarily frightened. Finally, a good whiff of what is heading their way will positively identify the intruder.

No matter how quiet and sneaky wolves or bears might be, they can't hide their scent. This is the final trigger that may send the tawny herd thundering through the meadow. Of course, an elk needn't see or hear a wolf or mountain lion if it can smell it. If scent is sometimes the final mark on the "flee checklist," it often also serves as a first defense when a predator is careless enough to let its scent drift toward the elk herd. Elk would just as soon not get a really good look at a wolf.

Despite all these early warning systems, perhaps the most important advantage a herd animal has over predators is simply that there are so many of them in one place at one time. Those in the center of the herd, for instance, certainly enjoy more safety than those near the edge. And even if a predator is successful, it can only take down one elk at a time. The odds are in the favor of the many. An elk in a herd is only one of many potential meals.

## COAT

No matter where they live all elk look pretty much alike, with the exception of size differences from region to region. But elk look noticeably different than other North American deer, and the difference isn't just in their size. Elk pelage (coat of hair) is distinctively contrasting, unlike that of white-tailed or mule deer which tends to gradually blend from darker to lighter areas and is more uniform overall.

For instance, the head and neck of an elk—called a mane and found on both males and females—is dark brown. In mature bulls, this portion of the coat can be very nearly black in color.

This dark mane gives way abruptly at the shoulder, where the coat becomes a tawny tan, a color carried across its withers, ribs, flanks and rump. On some animals there is a darker stripe down the spine. Legs are also quite dark—nearly as dark as the neck.

The summer coat shows less contrast, and the color is more a burnished copper.

Northern elk tend to be darker than those in warmer areas. The light coat of the Tule elk helps reflect solar energy—it keeps it cooler. The dark coat of northern elk soaks in solar energy—it keeps it warmer.

While this contrasting coat seems to be an adaptation making elk visible to each other when in the open, it also acts as effective camouflage in a forest setting.

The brightest area on all elk is its rump patch, which can be nearly white in color, though it might best be described as buff. When seen from the rear, it is shaped sort of like an upside down tear drop with two dark tails that run part-way down each leg. In the center is the elk's short tail, which is the same color as the patch. Depending upon the animal's age, and in which region it is found, the lower portions of the patch may be outlined in a dark brown stripe.

It was the elk's rump patch that gave it its other common name—wapiti—a word from the Shawnee that means "white rump." Just why this patch is so light in color is hard to say. It may serve as a means of

Elk molt twice a year, in spring and autumn.

spotting each other at a distance (no disadvantage as far as hiding from predators is concerned because a healthy elk can outrun them), and it may help elk keep track of each other in a hell-bent-for-leather run from danger. Sort of a means of following the leader in a dusty stampede or when fleeing in low light.

Elk have two coats—one for winter and one for summer—and twice a year they shed every single hair on their bodies. The longer guard hairs in both seasons' coats are hollow, although the summer hairs are much denser and shorter. The inside of each hair looks much like a honey-comb when viewed through a microscope. All those millions of little pockets trap warm air and slow convective heat loss, increasing its insulative qualities.

As effective as these hollow hairs are as insulation, the winter coat is further improved with a dense woolly undercoat. In fact, researchers estimate that the winter coat is five times warmer than the summer version, providing excellent protection from winter's harshest weather. It is so effective at trapping body heat that elk so adorned can sometimes be spotted laying down or browsing with a fresh, unmelted snowfall coating their backs. In addition, elk can make their hair stand on end to increase thermal efficiency, even the short hairs on their muzzles. Tiny muscles called "arrector pili" raise the hair in the same process that humans undergo when we get "goose bumps." We just no longer have the hair to erect.

The most obvious shedding takes place in spring—a relative term in elk country since spring-like weather can arrive as late as June at high elevations or in the far north. The most exposed areas shed first, and elk take on a very bedraggled look. Fall shedding also occurs, but because the short summer coat is being replaced by a longer, denser winter coat, the process is much less noticeable to the observer.

Both the timing of shedding and coat growth is determined largely by photoperiod—the amount of sunlight in a 24 hour period—rather than temperature. However, growing such a protective coat diverts energy away from other organs, and the elk's metabolism does a delicate balancing act during the two times a year it must molt.

The elk's rump patch gave it the Shawnee name *wapiti*, meaning "white-rump."

For instance, lactating cows will the be the last to shed their winter coat in the spring, putting the energy that would have gone into growing new hair into creating milk for their calves. Bulls also divert great stores of energy to the growing of antlers, sometimes at the expense of their winter coat. Reproduction is paramount even to survival, and some bulls enter the winter with a poor coat thanks to the rigors of the rut and the demands of growing a large rack. Fortunately for both cows and bulls, the demands of milk production and antler growth take place during the season of abundant foods.

## SIZED FOR SURVIVAL

Elk are among the world's largest deer, and the difference in size between males and females is less than in some other red deer subspecies where the difference in size is pronounced. The similarity in size between bulls and cows is probably due to the elk's herd lifestyle. In order for predators to capture their prey, they must first separate it from the herd, which is not easy to do, and the last thing any herd member wants. Usually, they capture a straggler, one that is injured or ill.

Evolution has tried to ensure that each elk is as strong and fast as the others in the herd (you only have to be faster than one other herd member to escape!). Since elk herds consist of cows, the calves of the year, and yearling (last year's) calves, and since male calves aren't evicted from the herd until the fall of their second year, elk cows evolved to be nearly as large as the yearling bulls. Their size also allows cows to compete effectively with the yearling bulls for forage. Cow elk even look a little like bulls—they have throat manes—whereas the female red deer does not.

The nutritional demands of growing both a new coat and new antlers require the lush forage of spring.

Next Page: Cow elk are nearly as large as the young bulls with which they must compete.

Among deer, only the caribou has taken this one step further, for cows even grow antlers as large as those of yearling bulls.

Still, if cow elk are as big as yearling bulls, they are not as big as bulls of their own age. Mature cows weigh between 400 and 600 pounds, while mature bulls generally weigh between 600 and 900 pounds. Occasionally, bulls can top 1,000 pounds (only the moose is a larger deer), and again, following Bergmann's Rule, the farther north you go in the elk's North American range, the larger they are. Age is a factor, obviously, but growth isn't always upward. While elk are among the fastest growing of this continent's animals (a calf can go from 35 pounds at birth in the spring to 225 by its first autumn, and 475 by its second), beyond a certain ripe old age, elk begin to lose weight. Aged cows and bulls, perhaps hindered by worn teeth and an inability to "get around" as well as they used to, shrink slightly as they find it difficult to obtain and consume enough food.

The elk's relatively large body is also a cold weather survival adaptation. Large bodied animals have lower metabolic rates than small bodied animals, and so can last longer in cold weather on the same amount of stored fat. Over the centuries of life in cold climates, nature has selected the largest elk to survive—and of course, only the survivors breed. Thus, elk are a race of very large deer.

## HERD HIERARCHY

Being big requires lots of food, and in order for an elk to acquire its typical twelve pounds of forage per day, it must feed in a place where the plants are relatively dense. If an elk had to feed in a thick forest, like a white-tailed deer, moving from one pocket of plants to another, there simply wouldn't be enough time in a day to eat all it needs. Most elk are active about ten to twelve hours per day, and most of that time

The best quality food is found in open areas
such as meadows and forest openings.

is spent looking for, and eating, forage plants. Therefore, the best place
for an elk to find both the quantity and quality of food it needs is in
meadows, forest openings and on grasslands. These locations might
change from time to time, and with the seasons—warmer, low elevations in winter; cooler, moist places in summer—but they are all
characterized by their openness.

In order to feed safely in the open, it is to an elk's advantage to do
it in the company of other elk. Evolving into a herd animal required
some psychological modifications. Herding is inherently social, and a
society requires rules. Too much energy would be diverted from feeding and caring for calves if the whole day was spent quarreling with
neighbors. Herd animals need peace.

Elk herds are led by a dominant matriarch.

A peaceful structure is enhanced by having a leader, and so elk herds are generally led by a matriarch. Old and wise, she knows the routes from one good food source to another, and the path to take from wintering to summer territories. These secrets are the result of learned behavior—knowledge she gained when following the old cows that led the herd in her youth. Obviously, in order to obtain this rank, a cow must be big, strong and intelligent—just the kind of cow that nature would also select to be a good breeder. Thus, many of the younger cows in the herd will be her daughters and granddaughters.

Other older cows seem to help share this responsibility too, which probably lends status for them and their offspring.

Status in an elk herd has definite advantages. Evidence indicates that the most dominant cows get to eat first when food is scarce, get to choose the best source of food even when abundant, and are allowed to select the best and safest bedding sites. These are huge advantages both in survival and at increasing one's odds to reproduce successfully, or while caring for young.

Although it is the desired norm, life in a herd isn't always peaceful. Dominant animals didn't get that way without challenge, and they don't stay that way without reinforcement. Such challenges, however, must remain infrequent, or the whole herd would always be in an uproar of competition, constantly bickering and wasting precious energy. To reduce conflict, elk have evolved a language of postures.

Like the pecking order among dogs or wolves in which the dominant animal displays its rank through raised tail and hackles, a dominant elk will indicate its status with ears laid flat, bared teeth, wide eyes and flared nostrils. Scientists call this "agonistic" behavior. Usually the subordinate animal recognizes this threat, but if it continues the challenge, the dominant cow will flail out with one forelimb. When near equals meet and refuse to capitulate to such threatening stares and kicks, they will rear up on their hind legs and "box" each other.

Next Page: The herd requires social structure and stability in order to survive and thrive.

Although it looks a bit humorous, boxing is anything but funny. Elk are powerful animals, with hooves both hard and sharp. A good thunking with those hooves can cause injury.

Such contests aren't relegated to just challenges to herd leaders. All down the pecking order, elk test each other. A young cow that would not dream of challenging a matriarch may behave quite belligerently toward another cow her own age. It might not be too far-fetched to say that each challenge is very important since taken cumulatively, those elk that are frequent "winners" will likely move up the ladder. In the wild, high ranking animals eat better, rest better, and breed more often—the very definition of success if the goal in life is to pass on your genes.

When moving from place to place, especially in the winter through snow, elk walk in single file, often following the matriarch. The lead cow communicates with the herd through a series of high pitched chirps and mews. Vocalization helps to keep the herd cohesive, and is also used between a cow and her calf.

Noises serve other purposes, too. If a threat is perceived by any herd member, it utters a loud alarm bark, which brings the herd to a state of attention, and can eventually send it scattering. When fleeing it may be every animal for itself for the first few seconds, but elk

Bulls of near-equal size band together in
herds of their own after the rut.

quickly regroup behind the leader. If a predator is to be successful,
it must quickly separate an animal from the herd during this moment
of confusion. Those elk that are injured, ill, or heavily pregnant are at
a disadvantage in a herd since they can't flee as quickly as the others and
quickly become targets. It should come as no surprise then that these
animals usually leave the herd to live a more secretive life of hiding.

Elk have been known to actually mob predators—particularly coyotes—relentlessly chasing them out of the vicinity. And just because a predator has been spotted doesn't mean the herd will take flight. Running away at every frightening sign would be a waste of energy. Elk herds remain cautiously alert as long as the threat doesn't enter its "flight distance"—the magical, unseen line beyond which the threat dare not cross without sending them galloping away.

When elk do flee, they often run great distances, and if disturbed too often in one area, simply avoid it. This has serious implications for elk in our increasingly altered world. Roads and development can cause elk to feel threatened, eventually causing them to flee even though adequate habitat may remain. Some elk have been pressured into abandoning their seasonal migrations, sometimes with disastrous results for the herd.

## Bulls

In winter, bulls of near equal size often gather in herds to make use of all the advantages herding behavior offers the cows and yearlings. And just like the cow herds, bull herds need some sort of societal rules to avoid constant bickering and wasting energy. Bulls do this by establishing dominance and submission based on size and antler mass.

Antlers help bull elk figure out dominance using a behavior called "sparring"—not to be confused with the battles that can occur during mating season. Instead, sparring is less heated and more ritualized.

Bull elk use sparring matches to determine rank.

Sparring is designed to avoid injury and cost as little energy as possible. In fact, the very shape of the bull elk's antlers help to lower the risk of injury. Designed to catch the opponent's rack rather than to spear him, the rivals' racks entwine in relative safety. Rarely occurring between greatly disparate bulls (unlike whitetails, where big bucks often "humor" young bucks with sparring matches), these sparring contests usually involve two elk of similar size that slowly approach each other with eyes averted. They almost appear nonchalant, as if they don't see each other, but you can be assured that they are sizing each other up. Before physical contact is made, they bob their antlers in a mirror image of each other, then lower their heads to engage antlers. This bobbing of heads allows each bull to once again assess his rival before committing to a sparring contest.

Next Page: Elk antlers are designed to catch an opponent, not spear him.

Cows choose their bull, not the other way around.

Once they commit to sparring and antlers are entwined, a wrestling match occurs—they twist their necks, shove each other around, and try to evade the other. This ritualized testing reaffirms each bull's status, and the subordinate animal is allowed to save face by simply moving backward, indicating an end to the match. Separating slowly, there is little sign of submissiveness, even by the "loser." Each elk walks away with a good appraisal of his sparring partner. No doubt he'll remember his look and smell, and if encountered during the rut, the losing bull may think twice before challenging the winner to a real dominance battle.

Sparring keeps the bull herd at peace through the winter, allowing them to concentrate on feeding and survival. Because this hierarchy is so important to peace, and because peace is important to survival, and because sparring with antlers is the process that controls it all, bull elk keep their antlers until about March.

Contrast this with forest-dwelling New World deer like the white-tail, which casts his antlers in January since he has absolutely no need to retain status. He's a loner, fending for himself in the forest. The only time he needs a status symbol is during the mating season. Once bull elk do cast their antlers, however, they leave the herd and retreat to thicker cover where each individual can hide.

Everything elk do—young, old, male and female—is merely a step toward reproduction. If you don't breed, you're a genetic dead-end.

Herding is an advantage most of the time, and so a social order is necessary to bring peace to a herd. But when it is better to be alone, when the odds of survival are enhanced by being single and secretive, elk have no qualms about assuming that lifestyle.

Cows move off by themselves to give birth, and bulls retreat to find the needed extra browse to grow antlers or to find peace from what would be an disorderly society after antlers are shed.

# CIRCLE OF
# LIFE

While there are many moments both grand and ordinary in the life of all creatures, there is one thing that is common to all, one thing that drives them all and toward which every action—eating, drinking, hiding, running—is but a step along the way: the need to pass on one's genes.

Although the ordinary motions are just that—ordinary—they are no less important than the grand spectacles, or ridiculous efforts, employed in seeking mates and reproducing. It is true that the most elaborate rituals of all animals are employed in mating. It is also true that such efforts are the culmination of eons of natural selection through which species find ways to ensure that the biggest, brightest, most fit specimens reproduce, and that the unfit are winnowed from the stock. The selection process is influenced by animals within a species—through competition throughout the year for food, shelter and safety, as well as through competition for mates—and is also influenced from outside the species. Predators help shape a prey species,

A young bull's first rut will follow
the growth of his first antlers.

as does weather and topography. The end result leaves the unfit dead, the near-fit still in the running, and the fittest at the top, ready to reproduce.

The reproductive cycle of the elk is magnificent at two times of the year: in the competition for mates during the autumn process called "the rut" and again in the spring and early summer as cows give birth, guard their young, and bring them into the herd. Of the two, the first is most spectacular to the human observer. Each step through every season is but one stride toward the completion of the cycle of birth and death.

## ANTLERS

When the hoarfrost clings to the sagebrush, when the bracken has browned and wilted, when the aspen leaves get tossed about by chill winds like snow in a gust, the mating season of the elk is in full drama. But long before the peak of this passion play the rehearsals have begun, responding to the intricacies of sunlight and hormones.

It is hard to pick an exact date as to when the cycle of the rut begins, and for cows and bulls the timing is different. But photoperiod, and its affects on the hypothalamus and the manufacturing of hormones, governs it. For most elk, the actual rut begins in late August or early September.

But you might also say that bull elk begin their reproductive cycle in the spring, even late winter, with the lengthening of days. This may be outside the commonly thought of time frame for elk reproduction, but consider that once the bulls shed their antlers in late winter, they immediately begin to grown new ones. Antler size and symmetry are essential components of a bull's desirability for, and ability as, a breeder.

Bulls advertise their status and readiness to breed
using impressive antlers and by bugling.

Large and flashy, antlers attract mates and intimidate rivals. As
weapons, they serve as tools to fend off rivals and protect the harem.
Combined with large body size, they are the coup de grace in the elk
selection process. In other words, although the actual rut occurs in the
fall, a bull can't be competitive without his antlers, the growth of
which begins in spring.

Antlers are fascinating things. Unlike horns, which are dead tissue
and permanent, antlers are living tissue that grow and are shed annually.
Antlers are recognized as some of the fastest growing tissue in the
animal world. The massive racks that elk grow start from nothing and
mature in just four months.

Antler growth begins from the pedicles, which are specialized parts of the forehead. Stimulated by the hormone testosterone, antlers are actually living bone, in which blood is supplied via a complex of tiny capillaries. While they grow, antlers are covered in "velvet"—a soft, fuzzy, blood-rich tissue that is akin to skin, even to the degree that it has sweat glands. In late summer to early autumn, the antler bone mineralizes and hardens, halting the blood flow. Racks are at full size, and no longer need the velvet and the blood flow it supplies. The velvet dies and over a twenty-four-hour period, bulls thrash it from their new, hard, white antlers. During this process, bloody surfaces are exposed, and the blood, in combination with the juices of the plants and trees the bull is now thrashing, stains the antlers in shades from mahogany to coffee. Only the tips remain ivory, gleaming like a newly risen moon. Once their antlers are freed of velvet, bulls begin searching for cows.

Each normal elk antler consists of a main beam with several branching tines. Bulls continue to grow larger and larger racks with each successive season, providing their health remains good and they have access to nutritious forage. Again, antlers are a visible sign of his fitness to reproduce—big antlers indicate vitality, symmetrical antlers indicate health, and since neither occurs without good nutrition, large, uniform antlers also indicate he is a smart survivor, able to seek out and acquire nutritious browse.

Each year the diameter of the pedicle increases, and it is the pedicle that determines antler diameter and size. Testosterone not only triggers the beginning of antler growth, it also induces mineralization and velvet shedding. And it is testosterone, or actually the lack of it, that causes antlers to be cast off sometime between mid-January and mid-April. A bull drops both antlers within a twenty-four-hour period a day or so after the bridge between the living pedicle and antler dies from a lack of testosterone.

As the rut begins, bulls shed the living skin known as "velvet" from their now-hardened antlers.

Abnormal antlers, those with odd branches or twisted tines, are usually the result of injury while they were still forming during the velvet stage. However, some irregular antlers, often called non-typical antlers, are genetic in origin. Usually the difference between these types can be discerned by how uniform the irregularities appear. Odd deformities to just one antler is the result of injury; irregularities that occur in both antlers—such as palmation (flat areas like those found in moose antlers) are probably due to genetics or diet.

## THE RUT

Adorned in antlers, the bull elk in rut is ready to convince cows that he, and he alone, should be allowed to breed with them. In elk, it is the cow that selects the mate, choosing from all the displaying bulls the one with which they will join. Bulls must do all that they can to attract then hold them. Like a Madison Avenue public relations firm, bull elk are masters of advertising, and they go to rigorous extremes displaying themselves. It is a passion play of enormous energy.

Timing, as they say, is everything. Should a bull elk come into rut too early, he will waste energy chasing cows that are not yet ready to

The most successful breeding bulls are those
that carefully tend their harem cows.

breed. By the time they are receptive, he will be worn out, and probably will have been replaced by a bull whose timing was better. In fact,
in some warm locations, cows are tended by a succession of bulls
because the rut is a longer, more drawn out affair. But where weather
is severe in winter, not only must the bull's timing be right on, so must
be that of the cows.

Dominant bulls find little time to rest during the rut.

The bigger the animal, the larger the offspring, and so the longer the gestation period. Elk are big deer, and their pregnancy is a drawn out affair. With an eight-and-a-half-month gestation period, mating must occur so that cows give birth to calves at just the right time. Cows that ovulate too late in the autumn produce calves late in the spring—too late to achieve full growth before the coming of the next winter, reducing the calf's chances of survival. Cows that ovulate too early drop calves before winter has fully loosened its cold grip, exposing the newborns to late storms and death that comes with it.

Natural selection then is working constantly on both sexes, winnowing the unfit from the herd. The higher the altitude, or more northern the latitude, the more critical the timing and the shorter the rut.

Thus, the elk mating season begins early in the autumn, perhaps even as early as late August, while that of smaller deer (with shorter gestation periods) doesn't occur until November.

Having ignored the cow herds over the summer, bulls are now like hormone-enraged teenagers that suddenly become aware of the opposite sex. Bulls are capable of breeding at two years of age, but the prime bulls are seven to twelve years old. Older, mature bulls handle the situation differently than young, inexperienced bulls. The latter are actually abhorred by cows, since they are constantly wanting to breed. Cows are, in addition to preparing to mate, larding up for winter. They need to put on the stores of fat that will sustain them and their fetus. They want peace, and they want to feed, and harassment by young bulls distracts them. They are receptive to the overtures of mature bulls because these old warriors will fend off all suitors, giving the cows relative security.

Autumn is a tough time for spike bulls. They are booted out of the herd to avoid inbreeding with relatives, chased away by the mature bulls that court the cows. Even if big bulls would tolerate them, the cows won't, wanting nothing to do with these suddenly sexually active teenagers. Spikes must strike off and fend for themselves now for the very first time in their lives, although they are allowed to rejoin the cow herds after the rut.

## BUGLING AND SCENT MARKING
With the coolness of September, mature bulls are actively strutting their stuff—both audibly and visibly. To draw attention to themselves, bulls bugle. The volume and pitch of their call determines how far it will carry—and the farther it carries, the larger the potential number of mates that may hear it. Bugling is an audible challenge to other bulls, too.

It serves to warn off competitors, although it is just as likely to attract them. Bull size is also important to bugling, since the bigger the chest, the more resonant and deeper the call. The high pitched bugle of elk is ideal for the unobstructed terrain in which elk live, for it carries farther than the low roar of the related red deer, whose call is better suited to thick forest. Following the end of their high pitched bugle, bull elk give off a yelping grunt, during which their belly twitches and they spray a stream of urine.

Urine is an important, though not completely understood, component of the bull elk's rutting routine. If nothing else, it is a scent "signature" since each elk's urine odor is as distinctive as are our fingerprints. With their acute sense of smell, being able to mark themselves so that another bull some distance away can recognize them may be an olfactory component of the bull hierarchy. After all, if you know the scent of a rival who has already defeated you, you can avoid him, saving both bulls the energy that would have been used trotting across hill and dale checking each other out. And it seems that scent would also play a role in keeping the harem together, since the cows will certainly imprint on the odor of "their" bull.

The bigger and more confident the bull, the more often he urinates on himself and in his wallows—muddy patches of earth in which he rolls. Most wallowing is done by these mature bulls, and they tend to favor the same wallows repeatedly, often lounging in them for hours. Bulls urinate copiously into the wallows, and on themselves. To spray himself with urine, a bull lowers his neck for a clear shot at it from between his legs. The thick, shaggy mane becomes an odor sponge. Bulls can control the flow in shape, producing either a fine spray or a steady stream. The scent of a rutting bull is so strong that even humans can smell them or their wallows. Since the biggest bulls spray the most urine and wallow more often, the smellier the male, it seems, the greater his odds of being chosen as a mate.

Rutting bulls douse themselves in the strong odors of urine and their wallows.

Scent glands located on the forehead and near the eyes probably impart important olfactory messages when rubbed on trees and branches.

## RUBBING

Bulls do a lot of rubbing during the rut. Not only do they rub their antlers on trees and use them to thrash bushes and grass (the clumps of grass caught in the antlers are thought by some to be a manner in which bulls make their antlers look larger), they rub their necks, faces and foreheads on trees. While it is well known that white-tailed deer bucks rub their forehead and preorbital (in front of the eye) glands on trees and rubs to leave their scent as a means of marking territory (and to let the does within that territory know they're available for breeding), it is unclear if bull elk rub for the same reasons.

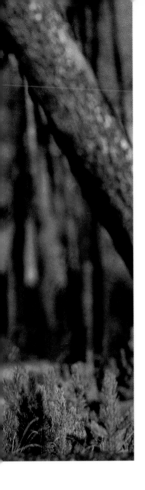

Scent glands release chemicals called pheromones—the olfactory alphabet of love—and the role they play in whitetail biology is much better understood than it is for elk. However, since bull elk can be seen frequently rubbing their preorbital glands on trees, as well as transferring mud from their manes to tree branches and trunks after rolling in their urine-rich wallows, scent must surely play some significant role.

And even if the elk's process or purpose is not exactly the same as the scent marking rituals of white-tailed bucks, it seems obvious that some kind of display or territorial marking is taking place. This is further evidenced by the fact that other elk, upon discovering a rub will check it out, often rubbing their own face and neck on it. It is anyone's guess, though, what they learn from the scent markings of bulls.

## RIVALS

In full rut, bull elk are big, smelly, and quite single minded creatures. Most of their day is spent in displaying, or in defending a harem of cows that they've gathered. Very little time is spent in feeding, and bulls lose a great deal of their stored body fat during the rut. If a rutting bull is overzealous, he can leave himself so worn and thin that he lessens his chance of surviving the coming winter.

If the bull elk's strategy is to display to, gather, then breed as many cows as possible, the cow's strategy is to select a suitable, vigorous mate, then let him defend her from rivals.

Next Page: The bull that gathers the largest harem will be the most successful at passing on his genes.

Even cows that have already joined a harem appear to be curious about checking out other bugling bulls, so the harem bull must out-compete his rivals to retain his cows. He must continue his vigorous displaying so that his cows don't begin to take him for granted, since other bulls will be vying for their attention. If he can't out-bugle his rivals, he attempts to quiet them—that is, defeat them in battle. Cows will only remain with a bull if he is obviously the finest of the lot. Frankly, for them its a buyer's market.

Bulls know this, and besides bugling and displaying, they physically try to keep cows from wandering off to find a better mate. If a cow wanders too far from the harem, the bull trots rapidly ahead of her and turns her back with the aid of his antlers—sometimes even striking her with them. But his best defense from losing her is to merely be the best suitor and defender, so he wears himself ragged in that pursuit. The most dangerous and energy intensive effort goes into driving off competing bulls.

When rivals meet, it isn't to either bull's advantage to walk away with significant injuries, whether loser or winner. Evolution has provided elk with a ritual display first, giving time to back off.

To convince a rival to back down, bull elk first show off. As they approach each other, the rivals often stop, thrash small trees and bugle. Often they'll trot, side by side in a "parallel march," continuing their bugling and smashing of small trees, even spraying urine. Each bull is now carefully assessing the other. At this point, one or the other may think twice and retreat, but if the contest is to continue, they slowly complete the approach, each seeking the uphill position to gain the advantage of gravity should a battle ensue. It seems that as soon as one bull senses the other is a bit "off guard" he turns on him and charges.

Rival bulls often thrash small trees or brush
as a prelude to a battle.

Meeting the charge, the rival locks antlers with his attacker. What
follows is a battle of sheer strength, which reveals why body size is so
important. If a bull can gain the uphill advantage, he can use his
weight and momentum to drive the opponent down, at which point
the battle will be quickly won.

Full-fledged dominance battles last only minutes, but they are long
minutes! No energy or effort is spared, and when a bull decides that
he's better off leaving, his troubles aren't over. Now he must find some
way of disengaging without leaving himself open to spearing by the
other's antlers.

When bulls in bull herds spar, they allow their sparring partner
to disengage by simply stepping back, without fear of retribution.
But during the rut, no such niceties are observed. If he can, the loser
turns quickly and runs, leaving only his rump exposed to danger.
And the victor will attack. Bulls frequently gore their opponents, and
in the course of the rut, most bulls acquire between thirty and fifty
antler wounds.

Next Page: Bulls must also guard against
the escape of cows from their harem.

Battles aren't just machismo; they are nature's way of ensuring only the fittest breed.

Dominance battles are serious encounters for many reasons. Losers (and winners) may be gored or otherwise injured so severely that they'll not survive. Victors go on to mate, fulfilling their genetic fate. Losers, at least for the time being, become genetic dead ends.

All the feeding, all the survival strategies, everything a bull has done in the past year to prepare himself for the role of breeder is wrapped up in those minutes in battle. It is easy to understand then why they spare no effort.

## MATING

Having defended his harem, the successful bull must now court his cows. When a cow is in estrus—a very short period lasting only twelve to fifteen hours—and is ready to mate, she'll allow the bull to approach her from behind. He does this with a head-up posture to signify his intent (a head down posture is more aggressive—the one he uses to drive her back into the harem if she strays—and so he avoids it now lest he frighten her).

Cow behavior changes only slightly as her heat period nears. She licks her flanks more often, feeds less, gets aggressive toward other cows, and generally hangs around the bull. He, in turn, spends more time with her, sometimes licking her body.

If the bull is young and inexperienced, a cow in estrus may actually court him, encouraging him by licking his face, neck and rear, and rubbing along his body. Although a cow would prefer not to mate with such an inexperienced bull, she may have no choice when older bulls are not available.

The cow in estrus will now tolerate the bull's courting moves, where she might have actively avoided him only a day earlier.

If the bull can lay his head on her rump and find her receptive to that move, he knows it is time to mate. He rears up and jumps forward, the cow taking most of his almost thousand pounds on her back. When she has been bred, the cow urinates, and although the entire episode takes but the briefest moment, it is the culmination of the entire rigorous rut. If she is successfully bred, she'll resume a nice, quiet life. If not, she'll come into heat in about three weeks, giving her another chance to reproduce for the year. Some cows even come into estrus a third time.

Cows begin breeding at two years of age, and depending upon locale, some cows continue to bear young until they are twenty years old. Reproductive success, however, drops once she's past fourteen years of age. Still, that's a remarkably long reproductive life, and one can easily see that herd reproductive rates are determined by the number of cows, not the number of bulls, since one bull can breed many females.

For the bull, the effort isn't over. Other cows await him. The rut is a long, drawn out, wearisome affair for him. Beginning in September, mountains and valleys reverberate with this lust for life through the auburn splendor of autumn. As October ends, the bull's testosterone level gradually drops. He becomes less interested in chasing cows and clashing with competitors. After nearly two months of non-stop carousing and thrashing, bulls turn to feeding again. Winter awaits, to take its toll on tired bulls and pregnant cows. But it is not in the plan that all should fail. For the strong, spring will see the fruits of the rut blossom in the warmth of a new sun.

## Birth

Thin and angular, elk in spring drift from their winter range to summer haunts, looking for and feeding on the tender shoots of bluegrass, brome and wheatgrass. Coats matted and dull, they had come through the rigors of winter safely, although the weak and the old now lay as tatters and bones in the meadows. Valleys, low, gray and wet with winter seared forage lays behind them, the lush sprouting forbs and grasses of the greening mountain meadows calling.

New spring grasses and forbs will enable elk to regain
the strength they lost due to the rigors of winter.

Spring is a critical time for elk. Stores of body fat are often completely depleted. Tough winters can leave elk looking like a bag of
bones, shoulder blades and hip bones poking from loose, draping
hides. A late storm now could spell disaster, driving even those that
had survived so long past the point of no return. Starvation occurs far
more often in the spring that it does in winter. In many ways it is the
most dangerous time of the year for the herd.

Not only is spring weather critical to the present herd, it can dic-
tate its future as well. Cows, pregnant the winter through, are nearly
ready to give birth. The developing fetus has sapped much of her energy,
demanding nutrition no matter the weather. During the peak of the
winter, the demands were relatively small, but as spring nears—in
April or May—the nutritional needs of the fetus climb dramatically.
Without adequate spring nutrition, a cow will give birth to a small calf,

and there is strong evidence that small calves grow up to be small adults with low social status in the herd. These, in turn, have poor luck finding mates. A tough spring may also mean that cows are unable to produce adequate milk, yet another cause in producing smaller-than-average sized calves. Thus, winters that drag out into spring can affect not only the adult animals of that year, but the future of the herd for years, yielding a poor return for the investment made by both cow and bull in mating.

Regardless of whether spring has been fair or foul, eventually the fruits of the rut will be born at least by some. For as surely as winter is cold, the weather will someday warm, and the heavily swollen cows will wander away, one by one, from the herd, leaving the barren cows and yearling bulls behind. Calving season, depending upon the altitude or latitude, arrives in late May or early June.

As they wander, cows search for the perfect calving site, a place usually located midway between the low altitude wintering grounds and summer's high haunts. But calving grounds aren't randomly chosen. Cows look for places that have good hiding cover for their offspring—fallen logs, brush piles, sagebrush, or bouldery, rough terrain—that are near water and good forage. As one would expect, such places are frequently found where two habitat types meet, such as where meadows abut forests.

Calves are playful; the play may also teach them something about their relative status in the herd.

Quietly and alone, the cow gives birth. Often she'll stand during the beginning of the miracle, turning to lick herself where the dark wet calf is emerging. Dropping to her knees, front-legs-first like a camel taking on a passenger, she lowers herself to the ground, then to her side. When the newborn emerges in the bright warmth of a spring day it is wet, weak and weighs between twenty and forty pounds. If it is lucky, if winter and spring and genetics have been kind to its mother, it will weigh in near thirty-five pounds and stand a good chance of surviving.

Next Page: Calves must soon learn to run swiftly so that they might join the protective herd.

A newborn calf takes its first hesitant steps.

## RAISING YOUNG

Now the reproductive investment of the cow has matured, and the check has been cashed. She carefully cleans the calf by licking it stem to stern and within a short time the rusty coated, white-spotted calf is dry and bright-eyed, ready to stand. Rising on wobbly legs, the calf is encouraged to leave the birth site, but not until the cow has consumed

all of the after-birth and blood-stained grass and earth, destroying the scent that would attract predators. In these early moments the calf bonds to its mother. The young elk must soon be able to join with, and run as fast as, the herd. Elk, therefore, produce a single calf that is born large and grows quickly so that it can fit into the herd.

Despite the fact that elk are herd animals, this portion of their lifecycle is much like that of non-herding deer like the whitetail. For a short time (about three weeks) cow and calf use the same "hider strategy" as other deer. Calves have little scent, and that scent is further minimized by staying put. If you don't wander around, you can't spread your scent. And if you don't move, you can't be seen. A spotted coat completes the strategy, providing good camouflage. As soon as the calf can walk the cow leads it away from the birth site to a safe hiding place, a location with good overhead cover, where she will leave the tender newborn.

If it seems strange that the cow would apparently abandon her calf, consider that a large cow can't hide nearly as easily as can the tiny calf. If she were to remain next to it, she'd merely be the forest equivalent of a highway neon sign proclaiming an all-night diner. Predators need only spot the cow to know that easy pickings await. In addition, the cow has come through both a long winter and pregnancy, only to face the even more energy consuming task of producing milk. She needs to feed, and feed a lot.

Because the calf is scentless and well hidden, the cow can move safely off to feed. The little one remains almost motionless, muscles rigid, head low, awaiting her return. The cow comes back very infrequently—only a few times a day—to check on the calf and to suckle it. She encourages it to defecate during this period, and may move the calf to a new, clean, odorless site before departing. But she is never too far away, and if predators do discover the calf, she'll reappear in a flash. Elk cows are courageous defenders of their young, and have even been known to face grizzly bears.

In fact, although adult elk can be, and are, killed by predators, most predation occurs on elk calves. Spring is a difficult time for predators, too, which are feeding their own young and are also trying to regain vigor after being tested by winter. Calves are far more vulnerable than adult elk, which are difficult to kill for small predators, like coyotes, and a fair challenge even for large predators. Coyotes, which frequently hunt alone or in pairs, have been known to gather into small packs in the spring just to take advantage of the bounty of young elk. While one or two coyotes distract the mother, the others sneak in to dispatch the calf.

But coyotes aren't the only predators that target elk calves. One Idaho study, in which fifty-three calves were radio collared, revealed that six were killed by mountain lions and twenty-eight were killed by

Cows only return at long intervals to suckle their calves.

black bears within the first few weeks of life. This is a startling statistic, and probably not typical, since the researchers found that bear density in this region was abnormally high during the study period. But it does reveal just what kind of odds a young elk may face during the critical period in which its only defense is to remain motionless.

Black bears and grizzlies employ a technique called the "slow search" when looking for calves. First of all, they just happen to be drawn to the same habitat as elk at this time for the same reason— these places are some of the first to green up—and since bears are omnivorous, they eat a lot of green veggies. Put into the same habitat, elk and bear are bound to cross paths. When bears encounter a lone cow, they just naturally figure that there must be a calf hidden somewhere nearby. If they can, they drive off the cow, and then methodically search the area for the calf. In many cases, they find it.

Of course, not every calf meets this fate, or there would be no more elk. Some escape merely by luck. But such randomness isn't the only factor at play. The wisest cows select the best hiding places, and thus, natural selection is at work. And even the calf's intelligence, or fortitude, plays a role, since when it avoids moving when predators are near, it increases its odds of survival. Lifting your head at the wrong time may satisfy your curiosity, but it may also be the very last thing you do.

After about three weeks of such Russian-roulette, hide-and-go-seek survival, elk calves are large enough to run swiftly. Now the cow can take her calf back to the herd where they can both enjoy its relative safety. A big hurdle has been cleared, although threats to the calf don't end now. Still, the odds have gotten significantly better, and both mother and child can focus on what needs to be done—eating.

Cows produce lots of nutritious milk for their calves, which nurse extensively for about two-and-a-half months. By the end of that time, calves are able to switch to grasses and shrubs, although some nursing continues. If a calf loses its mother during the nursing period, however, it is in for a tough time. Other cows will not allow it to nurse from them,

After they are able to run, calves can join the safety and protection of the herd.

Calves nurse for over two months. The rich milk is critical to ensure rapid growth to a size where the calf can survive its first winter.

since that would mean less milk for their own calf, lowering its odds of survival by stunting its growth. The abandoned calf probably won't starve—it will switch to forage. But without its mother's milk, its development will be slowed, which will show come winter when it is neither large enough or fat enough to survive.

Elk calves also face some acrimony in the herd, learning their hierarchic status. And because herds depend upon cohesiveness for survival, cow elk don't defend their young from belligerent herd members. To do so would cause strife, and the foremost rule of herd behavior is to maintain peace between members.

That doesn't mean that calves are in for too rough of a time. The elk herd, as a unit, sees the need to care for the young of all. The species benefits by high survival rates, and has evolved a strategy that allows for protection of the young and still gives cows the chance to feed enough to replenish their energy and produce adequate milk. The strategy is called a "nursery herd." A herd within the herd, it is like a daycare center. Various cows take turns baby-sitting the young of their peers, while the other mothers browse nearby with the rest of the herd. The calves follow this single cow, who adopts the responsibility for protecting them and guiding them out of trouble should it appear. When it does materialize in the form of fur and fangs, the cow flees, leading the calves away. The benefit of this strategy is fairly obvious. During a melee, calves need only focus on a single adult, which lowers the odds that they'll become confused and disoriented. And when the whole of the herd settles down after the threat, all the mothers gather at the nursery herd to sniff and listen to the calves to find their own.

Next Page: Elk form nursery herds so cows can feed while their young are supervised and protected.

By this time, summer is in its full lushness. Bulls are off on their own, already growing antlers, seeking the nutritious browse they need for that growth, and for the fat they must lay on for the coming rut. Days are warm, long and sweet, and so are the elk's foods, full of moisture and nutrition. Calves frequently romp in the sheer joy of youth. Aside from the annoyance of insects, once the calves are big enough to outrun predators, this is a time of peace and plenty for all elk. It is the time that shapes the elk, too. This is the time of seasonal abundance.

But summer is brief in elk country. In but a few short months, the whole array of the rut will again unfold as the cycle continues its endless rotation. As it has for ten thousand years, the elk herd will revel in the rut, face the challenge of winter, struggle through the late storms of spring, bear young with the waxing of summer

The cycle of life continues for elk.

and feed under the warmth of an August sun. Winter and spring will see some elk fade away, to join the earth or become the stuff that makes up those animals that prey upon them. The cycle of seasons is but a small loop in the big circle of life.

# A SHARED
# FUTURE

The habitats that are beneficial to elk, the fundamental elements that are necessary to elk survival, are necessary to humans as well. So if we need a selfish reason to preserve wild places and animals, this ought to be enough. We see this clearly when we look to our past, see how humans and elk coexisted in the same environs for tens of thousands of years, how the lands and waters and foods and animals that shaped the elk shaped us as well. Even into the fabric of our lives is woven the meandering tracks of elk. We need merely to view the cave paintings of ancient Europe depicting elk ancestors to know that elk have always been a part of our existence.

As the wolf and elk have a relationship, so do humans and elk. And until recently, our relationship with elk was based on the same sort of natural paradigm. Now, however, we are capable of straying outside that model, capable of altering even the evolution of this species. And I ask, do we have that right? We must have the wisdom and vision to see tomorrow.

This bull will look out for himself
if we look after protecting elk habitat.

But we can do without elk, just as they could do well without us. What we both can't do without are the mountains, the forests, the clean waters, the unpolluted air, the complex food web that sustains us.

Elk are less of a "canary in the mine shaft" than some species, but they do tell us something about the health of our land, and the fate of this species ought to tell us much about our own future and our humanity. Should we find that we do not care enough about elk and other wild creatures to provide a place on Earth for them to fulfill their fate, to complete their evolutionary path, we ought then to seriously question whether indeed we are worthy of the notion of superiority.

Things are pretty good in elk country right now. About a million elk roam the forests again, primarily in the West where large blocks of public lands provide habitat in varying degrees of suitability. But even in the West, human population grows, and conflicts are daily arising between the needs, or at least the wants, of humans and the absolute requirements of animals, elk included.

Elk are mobile, and tend to migrate between winter and summer habitat. It is not enough to save the hills and valleys in which they spend their summer, building roads, ranches, condominiums, towns, resort communities and homes where elk must spend their winter. Fragmentation of habitat is a serious problem, and elk simply do not have the option of moving elsewhere.

Our own humility and humanity will decide whether or not we will take their needs into consideration.

Saving habitat requires making choices. Tough choices. Amidst the cries of "jobs versus environment" that rallies around controversial

The elk rules over the wild lands with majesty and splendor.

timber sales, amidst the personal ambitions of politicians and developers, amidst the desires of city weary people to own a small piece of property where they can build a cabin or a home, must fall the needs of elk and other wildlife. Policy, and politics, will decide whether habitat is saved. And as we all know, politics is run by those who seek to determine its future. If those who care about elk are absent in the debates, so too then will be the needs of elk.

As elk enrich all our lives, we must
continue to enrich theirs responsibly.

Hours of effort, tons of money, and personal sacrifice have been the currency that has bought the research, the land, the political decisions, that bode well for the future of elk, a great deal of that altruistic effort funneled through the Rocky Mountain Elk Foundation, a group whose members are largely hunters. When we are unified by such groups, animals do have a voice in the decisions that will determine their future.

There are other problems. Game ranching in the West threatens wild elk with the importation of disease. Tuberculosis and other serious diseases from these game farmed elk/red deer hybrids has already

spread in some areas to wild deer and elk, where there is little chance of saving these animals, or curtailing its spread. Other problems can arise when these animals escape to the wild since many of them are red deer hybrids, capable of breeding with wild elk. The pollution of the elk gene pool by these escapees may cause significant and irreversible problems for elk, with potential for altering even their evolution. And the ranch fencing itself cuts elk off from its food sources and migration routes.

We have reached a critical juncture in elk management. Heroic efforts and good fortune saved elk from extinction and restored them to some abundance. The efforts that rescued them came from the heart, made by people with an admiration and passion for the species. Fortunately, there are still these kind of people working every day to continue the success.

However, millions of people will never hear an elk bugle. I wish they could. There is a primal majesty in that call that stirs the soul the way few other things can. I wish too that they could see elk country, to know its beauty and wildness, see that although we've done some horrible things to our planet, there are still places wild and lovely and in them the rituals and struggles of other living races goes on daily, blithely ignorant of our own concerns. For all is not gloom and doom. Ours is a beautiful planet, vibrant, lush, full of inspiration and capable of sustaining not only our bodies but our spirits as well. As far as I know, such planets are hard to come by. We ought to care for and enjoy this one.

The interesting thing about elk—and all animals—is that they just want to go about their business. Evolution has given them every tool they need to fight enemies, find mates, survive harsh weather, raise young. They know that the sun rises in the east so that they may find warmth in winter. They know that streams tumble from the hills so that they may drink from them. They know that valleys are free of snow in winter so that they may graze in them. Elk know all of these things and much, much more.

Millions of years have shaped the elk to be hardy and adaptive. It has its own society, its own language. But despite all of that, the pressures that elk will face in the future are outside of its circle of influence. They will eat and bear young, bugle and fight as they always have.

Everything else about their future is up to us.

The presence of an elk reminds us of the "wild" in wilderness.